CHRISTMAS SWEETS
and
HOLIDAY TREATS

Christmas Sweets AND Holiday Treats

Forty Vintage Recipes for Festive Cookies, Confections, and Other Delights

Allison Kyle Leopold

CLARKSON POTTER/PUBLISHERS

NEW YORK

Published by Clarkson Potter/Publishers, Inc., 201 East 50th Street, New York,
New York 10022. Member of the Crown Publishing Group.

Random House, Inc. New York, Toronto, London, Sydney, Auckland

CLARKSON N. POTTER, POTTER, and colophon are trademarks of
Clarkson N. Potter, Inc.

Manufactured in Hong Kong

Design by Mary A. Wirth

Library of Congress Cataloging-in-Publication Data

Leopold, Allison Kyle
Holiday treats: forty vintage recipes for festive cookies, confections, and other
delights / by Allison Kyle Leopold.
p.   cm.
Includes index.
1. Christmas cookery. 2. Thanksgiving cookery. 3. Confectionery—United States.
4. Victoriana—United States. I. Title.
TX739.2.C45L46   1995
641.5'68—dc20   95-3198
CIP
ISBN 0-517-59144-8

10   9   8   7   6   5   4   3   2   1

First Edition

FOR

Spencer and Justin

To Marie Baker-Lee, Marie Luise Proeller,
Grace Young, Joanne Leonhardt Cassullo, Deborah Geltman,
Mary A. Wirth, Lauren Shakely, and everyone at Clarkson Potter,
Thomas Cohen—and everyone who tasted and commented—
my appreciative thanks.

A Bright
and Happy
Christmas

CONTENTS

AUTHOR'S NOTE

Several years ago I fell in love with the spirit of Victorian holiday entertaining. Leafing through old cookbooks, intrigued by recipes with nostalgic names like Quaking Pudding, Codling Tarts, and Excellent Light Puffs, I began to experiment with these old-fashioned specialties for my own dinner parties and family celebrations. While all of the re-created dishes have been rewarding to make, the desserts and confections have been the crowd pleasers. Modern-day sensibilities are tempted by the dense and fragrant spice-laden cakes; the moist, baked puddings; the resplendent trifles and quaint cookies.

Of course, since foods and kitchen equipment—and, to a degree, tastes—have changed, the final recipes have involved some compromise and updating. Measurements

have been adjusted to 20th-century standards. Butter and cream have been cut back in concession to contemporary taste and health concerns. Occasionally, substitutions have been made for ingredients no longer commonly available.

Despite these alterations, I have found that Victorian cookery adapts quite nicely to today's kitchen—and to the demands of the busy 20th-century cook. After all, by the second half of the 19th century, a good deal of cookery was already done on a fancifully decorated iron cookstove rather than on an open hearth. These great iron contraptions were called *cookstoves* to differentiate them from the stoves used to heat the parlor. But since cookstoves lacked temperature controls and dials (the degree of heat was determined by the type and amount of wood burned), most period recipes are still imprecise and require a bit of translation. "Cook in hot oven till good and done" was a common enough direction in early 19th-century cookery guides.

These recipes have their origins in the 19th century, the years during which most of the rituals of our modern-day holidays originated. Some combine authentic information from several vintage sources; in others, the original has served as the springboard and inspiration. Elaborate as some of these recipes may initially appear, most are actually easy to prepare. All are part of our common celebratory heritage, reminiscent of the days when gathering in the home for feasting and merriment—and old-time cooking—were part of every family's tradition.

INTRODUCTION

THE HOLIDAY SEASON inevitably means a return to hearth, home, and family—a time for honoring old traditions and for creating new ones. For me it can be relining a cupboard in old-fashioned paper lace shelf edging or filling vintage oil lamps with scented oil in anticipation of the glow they will lend to holiday entertaining. At this time of year, Victorian houses—ours was built in 1882—seem to demand that kind of attention.

But whether your house is old or new, the holidays are a time for returning to ritual and tradition. Then as now, special foods were prepared, seasonal pastimes shared, and houses decorated with fragrant greenery, all traditions that hark back to the days of Queen Victoria.

In fact, we can credit the Victorians for making the holidays the true family festivals we know today. Americans of the Victorian era popularized the Thanksgiving feast with its turkey, stuffing, and pumpkin pie, and to the English Victorians we owe our Yule logs, wassail bowls, gingerbread cookies, and of course, the most visible sign of Christmas, the sumptuously decorated Christmas tree.

Early Victorian Christmas trees with their handmade ornaments differed from the opulent, late-century trees, glittering with the manufactured ornaments that had only recently become available. And on the American prairie, trees were more homespun, with gilded nuts, pinecones, molasses-and-popcorn balls, and carved wooden figures suspended from bits of ribbon or yarn.

Special foods, of course, always accompanied the holidays. During the 19th century, though, cooking and food preparation were more social experiences than they are today, and special occasions offered the opportunity for families and friends not only to celebrate but to share new skills, exchange recipes, and recount community news. In fact, people often traveled as far as twenty miles—a significant distance in those horse-and-wagon days—cheerfully lugging food and gifts, eager to show off the year's hard-won acquisitions: a handsome sleigh, a team of new horses, a fancy shawl from one of the new mail-order catalogs, even a thriving new baby born that spring. As for the hosts, their efforts involved prodigious preparation: preserving fruits, baking pies, preparing sweetmeats, and decorating the home with fresh-smelling greenery, beribboned baskets of sugared fruits, and other welcoming touches.

Long before Thanksgiving Day dawned, young boys would trudge down to the root cellar where winter vegetables like squash, parsnips, and turnips were stored. These were scrubbed, prepared for cooking, and kept ready in a cold place. Glistening cranberry jelly was made, apples wiped and shined, and raisins and nuts arranged in pretty dishes. Mince pies were laboriously prepared—these were thought to be better if kept at least a week after baking. Tarts, on the other hand, only needed to be baked the day before, along with flaky chicken pie, which was traditionally warmed up for noontime dinner.

Certain foods, of course, had already become indelibly associated with specific celebrations. By the 1870s, turkey was established as the quintessential Thanksgiving dish, as well as heartily approved for Christmas dinner, along with the English favorites roast goose and roast beef. Oysters, a symbol of luxury, were yet another menu staple. Both Thanksgiving dinner and Christmas dinner were served at three in the afternoon, after church attendance, a tradition that actually went back to the 18th century.

Regional differences in holiday menus naturally existed. On the Eastern Seaboard or in the growing urban centers, holiday feasts were different from those celebrated on the frontier, where the menu was still more immediately dependent on the harvest and the hunt. Many a company dinner on the Midwestern prairie was celebrated with stewed jackrabbit, cornbread spread with molasses—rather than more costly butter—and vinegar pie, which was similar to

lemon pie and common in areas where lemons were scarce.

But in every part of the country, a sumptuous dessert table was a tradition. Just as no Thanksgiving could be imagined without pumpkin pie, no Christmas could be complete without fruitcake and plum pudding—benchmarks of a homemaker's culinary skill. Other eagerly anticipated specialties were rich, cakelike puddings, elaborately molded desserts, gingerbread, and precious candied sweetmeats. During the 1860s, the diary of one little girl recalled the holiday storerooms and pantries of her home, filled not only with plum puddings and mince pies but with delectable oak-leaf cookies sprinkled with colored sugar, caraway comfits, and homemade peppermint drops, all of which arrived almost daily from family and friends. "At Christmas time, the kitchen wore a festive air somewhat akin to what one read about in the stories of Old England," she wrote. Since sugar was costly and not always available, sweets like these, along with sugarplums, popcorn balls, truffles, and Turkish Delight, washed down with multiple punch cups of wassail, mulled wine, and Yuletide punches, made festive occasions out of any gathering.

Fortunately for us, many favorite recipes from those times were enthusiastically recorded for us to rediscover and re-create today. What follows are those for some very special, romantic, yet thoroughly traditional desserts—all very approachable, and guaranteed to make dramatic and welcome additions to any holiday table, as well as welcome homemade gifts from the holiday kitchen.

A MERRY CHRISTMAS IS A DELIGHT TO HAVE; A GLAD CHRISTMAS IS A JOY, BUT A GOOD CHRISTMAS IS BEST OF ALL.—EDWARD W. BOK, 1890

PUDDINGS, FRITTERS, AND SPECIAL DESSERTS

SWEET OR SAVORY, boiled in a bag, steamed in a tin mold or earthen dish, or baked in an oven, puddings were once the 19th century's primary dessert, and became even more elaborate at holiday times when all the housewife's culinary skills were called into play. Pudding recipes included in this section represent a tempting mix of baked puddings, steamed puddings, and even a delightful frozen pudding.

Puddings were originally prepared by boiling the ingredients together in a cloth or pudding bag in a large pot over an open fireplace, a somewhat risky procedure since too much bread, too much flour or meal, or even tying the bag too securely could make a pudding heavy to the point of its being indigestible. Once homely pudding bags were replaced by all sorts of marvelous molds of tin or earthenware, and the oven took over the role of the fireplace, the common pudding became a more elegant dish, suitable for garnishing with fruit, cream, and fancy syrups. Beautiful antique pudding molds, some geometric, others patterned with fruits, vines, and leaves, can still be found today, although they are more useful for decorative purposes than for actual baking.

Other special desserts that found a place at holiday and company dinners are fruit-filled fritters, a more delicate version of our doughnuts or crullers; molded jellies, much like our gelatin molds today; rich Bavarian creams; and rum-soaked trifle, which was also known as tipsy pudding. Nor would any holiday dinner have been considered complete without the novelty of at least one frozen or chilled dessert. Creams, custards, ices, and snows were an expected part of the meal.

All of these holiday specialties are not only traditional but also splendidly romantic, especially when garnished with sprigs of greenery and mint, glittering glacéed fruits and sugared nuts, crystallized flowers or shaved chocolate swirls. Especially at holiday time, when presentation was— and is—an important part of the feast, these treats can turn a holiday dinner into a dramatic event when they emerge triumphantly from the kitchen.

TRY TO DISCOVER THE SPECIAL
WISH OF EACH CHILD'S HEART
AND GRATIFY IT. IF A DOLL IS
LONGED FOR, A BOOK WILL NOT
GIVE HALF AS MUCH PLEASURE
ALTHOUGH IT MAY HAVE COST
MORE.
—*MOTHER'S CORNER*, 1890

Baked Cranberry Pudding

Today's cultivated cranberries are larger, juicier, and sweeter than the wild cranberries of 100 years ago, but this recipe, inspired by several simple batter-and-cranberry sauce recipes from the 1880s, makes a delicious berry-laden and cakelike dessert that is not too sweet. Blueberries (frozen) or canned peaches, drained and sliced, can also be substituted, and still aptly evoke the flavor of the era.

To cook the cranberries, combine the sugar and water in a medium-size saucepan. Bring to a boil, then add the cranberries and the grated orange zest. Cook about 5 minutes, until the cranberry skins start to pop. Remove from the heat, let cool slightly, then pour into a greased 11 × 7 inch pan. Set aside. Preheat the oven to 350° F.

To make the batter, beat the whole egg and 2 yolks in a large bowl until smooth. Add ⅔ cup sugar and beat until smooth. Combine the flour, ½ teaspoon salt, baking powder, and baking soda, then add them to the egg-and-sugar mixture. Next, pour in the melted butter, milk, and zest and stir until smooth. Set aside. In a small bowl, beat the egg whites with a pinch of salt until soft peaks form. Slowly blend in the remaining 2 tablespoons sugar. Continue beat-

CRANBERRIES
- 1 c. sugar
- ¾ c. water
- 3 c. fresh or frozen cranberries
- 2 tsp. grated orange zest

BATTER
- 1 large egg
- 2 large egg yolks
- ⅔ c. plus 2 Tbsp. sugar
- 1¼ c. all-purpose flour
- ½ tsp. salt, plus extra for beating egg whites
- ½ tsp. baking powder
- ¼ tsp. baking soda
- ¼ c. (½ stick) unsalted butter, melted
- 3 Tbsp. milk
- 2 Tbsp. grated orange zest
- 3 large egg whites
- Vanilla ice cream or Lemon Sauce (recipe follows) to serve

ing until stiff but not dry peaks form, then fold into the batter mixture. Pour the batter over the pan of cranberries, smooth the top, and bake for 30 minutes until golden and the juices bubble up around the edges. Cool slightly, then scoop out of the pan with a large spoon, turning the pudding fruit-side-up in a dish. Serve with vanilla ice cream or Lemon Sauce.

Serves 8 to 10

Lemon Sauce

Combine the sugar and cornstarch in a saucepan. Add the boiling water and whisk until smooth. Cook on medium-high heat until boiling and the mixture thickens. Reduce the heat and cook 5 minutes, stirring occasionally. Remove from the heat. Add the butter and whisk until melted. Add the juice, zest, and nutmeg and whisk until blended.

Makes 2⅔ cups

⅔ c. sugar
2 Tbsp. cornstarch
2 c. boiling water
1½ Tbsp. unsalted butter, cut into small pieces
Juice and zest from 1 lemon
1½ tsp. ground nutmeg

Steamed Chocolate Pudding

This moist pudding, adapted from an 1880s recipe, is lighter than most cakes and moist and slightly puffy like a soufflé. It should be served immediately from the oven, as the grand finale to a meal, with fresh whipped cream and a few berries or, as the Victorians liked it, with meringue or raspberry sauce. Fresh mint leaves also make a pretty holiday garnish.

4 large eggs, separated
3 oz. semisweet chocolate, melted and cooled
½ tsp. almond extract
2 tsp. all-purpose flour
Pinch of salt
½ c. sugar
Whipped cream, meringue, or Raspberry Sauce (recipe follows) to serve

In a mixing bowl, beat the egg yolks until light. Stir in the cooled chocolate and the almond extract, then blend in the flour until well combined. Set aside. In a large covered pot boil enough water to come halfway up the sides of the mold while steaming. While it is coming to a boil, in another bowl beat the egg whites with a pinch of salt until foamy. Continue beating until soft peaks form, then gradually add the sugar. Beat until stiff but not dry peaks form, then fold into the chocolate mixture just until combined. Pour into a buttered 1½-quart soufflé dish and cover securely with foil, pressing the foil around the sides of the dish.

Place a rack in another large pot and set the soufflé dish on the rack. Add enough boiling water to come halfway up the sides of the mold. Cover the pot and bring the water back to a boil over medium heat. Steam 40 to 45 minutes

until the top of the pudding is puffed and an inserted skewer comes out dry. Remove from the steam pot and serve immediately with the desired accompaniment.

Serves 4 to 6

Raspberry Sauce

Combine the preserves, water, and lemon juice in a small saucepan. Bring to a boil, then reduce the heat and simmer 5 minutes. Strain, cover, and cool in the refrigerator. To serve, pour over individual servings of pudding and garnish with fresh mint leaves.

Makes 2⅔ cups

2 c. raspberry preserves
1 c. water
3 Tbsp. lemon juice
   Fresh mint leaves to
   garnish

Cabinet Pudding

An elaborate though easily assembled combination of simple sponge cake, flavored custard, and candied fruit, this classic dish, which was sometimes called Chancellor's Pudding, was a favorite in Queen Victoria's time. Because of its many steps and elegant appearance, Cabinet Pudding was considered ideal for a celebratory dinner or special tea. The following recipe for this regal dessert has been adapted from several vintage sources. Cake layers can be made in advance, then frozen until ready to use.

To make the cake, preheat the oven to 350° F. Butter a 15½ × 10½ × 1⅛ inch (or slightly smaller, not larger) pan, then line with wax paper that has been lightly buttered then floured. Set aside. In a medium-size bowl, beat the egg whites until soft peaks form, then gradually add the sugar until the peaks become stiff but not dry. In a separate bowl, beat the yolks until light, then add the orange and lemon zests and orange liqueur. Fold the egg whites into the yolks until just combined. Gently fold in the flour. Spread evenly in the prepared pan (the batter will be ½ to ¾ inch deep). Bake 10 to 12 minutes until light brown and the top springs back lightly when touched. Lower the oven temperature to

CAKE
4 large eggs, separated
½ c. sugar
1½ tsp. grated orange zest
1½ tsp. grated lemon zest
1 tsp. orange liqueur
1 c. sifted cake flour

FILLING
1½ c. orange marmalade
¾ c. chopped pistachios
3 Tbsp. candied lemon rind
(see recipe page 68, or available at confectionery and specialty stores and some supermarkets)
¾ c. finely chopped candied ginger

PUDDING
2 large egg yolks
½ c. sugar
¼ c. milk
¾ c. heavy cream
1 Tbsp. orange marmalade
1½ tsp. orange liqueur, Cointreau or Triple-Sec

325° F. Cool the cake 2 to 3 minutes on a rack, then invert, peeling off the paper carefully.

To assemble the cake, heat the oven to 325° F. Line a 2-quart soufflé dish with foil that has been lightly buttered. Cut three cake rounds, each the same diameter as the interior of the dish. It may be necessary to use two pieces and patch the center layer. Put the first layer in the bottom of the dish and spread thickly with ½ cup orange marmalade until covered completely. Sprinkle on ¼ cup of the pistachios, 1 tablespoon lemon rind, and ¼ cup candied ginger. Repeat with the other two layers, stacking them one on top of the other in the soufflé dish. Set aside.

To prepare the pudding, whisk the egg yolks with the sugar, then set aside. Next, heat the milk and heavy cream in a saucepan until small bubbles form, and pour gradually over the yolk mixture, whisking constantly. Pour the custard back in the pan and cook over medium-low heat, stirring constantly until it coats the back of a spoon. Do not let it boil. Remove from the heat and stir in the marmalade and orange liqueur. Then slowly pour the pudding over the cake, pressing the edges of the cake away from the sides of the soufflé dish with a spatula so the custard will coat the sides. Set the dish in a large baking pan filled with water that comes halfway up the sides of the dish, and bake for 1 to 1¼ hours, until the top is golden brown. Cool to room temperature, then refrigerate until ready to serve (this can be made the day before serving). Unmold and garnish as desired.

Serves 6 to 8

GARNISH
Crushed macaroons, whipped cream, citron or orange slices, or candied or fresh flowers, as desired

STEAM LEFT-OVER PLUM PUDDING INTO INDIVIDUAL PORTIONS FOR DAY-AFTER-THANKSGIVING GUESTS. —*THE MODERN PRISCILLA*, 1908

Golden Plum Pudding with Fresh Fruit & Apricot Nectar

Traditionally, this rich, brandy-soaked fruit-and-spice mixture is made with currants, raisins, sultanas, candied or dried fruits, and beef suet or lard. During the 19th century, more elegant versions substituted preserved ginger and more refined conserves. This unique plum pudding, modeled after an 1861 recipe by Mrs. Isabella Beeton and made with *fresh* fruit and apricots, is a lovely surprise—similar enough to appeal to plum pudding devotees, yet different enough to intrigue abstainers. It produces a beautifully golden pudding studded with fresh apples and pears. Although cloth-wrapped plum puddings were ball-shaped, this one looks most impressive when prepared in a decorative mold inverted, and passed with Hard Sauce.

1 tart apple, cored, chopped, and peeled
1 sweet pear, cored, chopped, and peeled
¼ c. golden raisins
¼ c. chopped candied orange peel
¼ c. diced dried prunes
½ c. chopped dried apricots
½ c. chopped blanched almonds
2 Tbsp. orange juice concentrate, thawed
2 Tbsp. lemon juice
½ c. brandy
½ c. apricot nectar
1¼ c. flour
1½ tsp. baking powder
¼ tsp. baking soda
¼ tsp. salt
10 Tbsp. (1¼ sticks) unsalted butter, softened
⅔ c. light brown sugar
3 large eggs
Hard Sauce to serve (optional; recipe follows)

Put a rack in the bottom of a large pot and fill with enough water to reach 2 to 3 inches up the side of a 2-quart mold. Bring the water to a boil. Butter the inside of a 2-quart mold.

Combine the apple, pear, raisins, orange peel, prunes, apricots, and almonds in a medium bowl. Stir in the orange juice concentrate, lemon juice, brandy, and apricot nectar.

Set aside. In another bowl, combine the flour, baking powder, baking soda, and salt. In a mixing bowl, beat the butter and brown sugar until light, then add the eggs one at a time, beating well after each addition. Add the flour mixture and beat 1 minute at medium-high speed. Add the fruit mixture and stir.

Pour the mixture into the buttered mold, filling it three-quarters full (leaving room to expand), and smooth the top. Secure the top of the mold and lower into the boiling water. Cover. Lower the heat so the water is at a simmer and steam is escaping from the lid of the pot. Steam for 2 hours, then remove the pot lid and lift out the mold, carefully unclamping its top. Let the pudding cool on a rack for 45 minutes to 1 hour. Run a knife around the inside edge of the mold and turn the pudding out onto the rack to cool completely. Serve sliced, with or without sauce.

Serves 8

To Flame a Plum Pudding

WARM 2 TO 3 TABLESPOONS OF BRANDY IN A SAUCEPAN OVER A LOW FLAME. POUR INTO A SERVING SPOON OR LADLE, IGNITE, THEN CAREFULLY POUR OVER THE HOT PUDDING.

Hard Sauce

This sauce is spooned onto the pudding rather than poured.

Thoroughly mix the butter, confectioners' sugar, brandy, and lemon juice in a bowl with an electric mixer. After slicing the pudding, place a dollop of sauce on top or on the side.

6 Tbsp. (¾ stick) unsalted butter, softened
2¾ c. confectioners' sugar
¼ c. brandy or rum
1 tsp. lemon juice

Clementine Fritters with Beehive Sauce

Apples, gooseberries, blackberries, peaches, and pineapple are all appropriate fruits for these dessert fritters, but oranges, once hard to come by in most parts of the country, are still the most desirable. This variation, inspired by an 1878 recipe, is made with clementines; mandarin oranges, tangerines, or navel oranges can be substituted.

Beehive Sauce to serve
(recipe follows)

Vegetable oil for frying
⅔ c. milk
2 large eggs
2 c. all-purpose flour
⅓ c. sugar
¾ tsp. salt
2 tsp. baking powder
4 clementines, peeled and sectioned
Confectioners' sugar for dusting (optional)

Prepare the Beehive Sauce before beginning the fritters. While you prepare the batter, begin heating the vegetable oil 2 to 3 inches deep in a medium saucepan to a temperature of 375° F. At that temperature, the fritter will seal and not become soggy while frying.

In a small bowl, combine the milk and eggs, beating well. In a medium bowl, combine the flour, sugar, salt, and baking powder, then stir in the egg mixture until completely combined. The batter will be thick. Stir in the clementine sections, coating them completely.

When the oil reaches the right temperature (if a thermometer is not available, test the temperature by dropping a bit of batter into the oil: if it spins and turns golden brown, the oil is ready), drop 2 to 3 coated clementine sections into the oil, turning them when the bottom side turns golden

brown (about 30 to 60 seconds). The fritters will resist turning until ready. After the second side is golden brown, remove with a slotted spoon to a plate covered with paper towels. Repeat with the remaining fruit sections. Dust with confectioners' sugar, if desired, and serve immediately with Beehive Sauce.

Serves 4

Beehive Sauce

Combine all the ingredients in a small saucepan. Warm over low heat and serve with fritters.

Makes 1½ cups

1 c. (2 sticks) unsalted butter, slightly melted
½ c. honey
2 Tbsp. orange juice concentrate, thawed
6 Tbsp. orange zest (more if desired)

English Pear & Chocolate Trifle

Rich with sherry, soft custard, jam, and cake, trifle is one of the most extravagant desserts—a Victorian tour de force. Its basic components are cake (usually sponge cake), soaked in sherry or other liqueur and then layered with jam, over which a richly flavored custard is poured. The whole is topped with whipped cream and garnished with berries, slivered almonds, glacéed cherries, and other confections. To show off the trifle's many layers, it is usually presented in an elegant cut-glass bowl or deep trifle dish.

Trifle was typically made with apricot, strawberry, or raspberry jam, and economical homemakers felt free to use stale cake—which was fully sanctioned by most of the cookery guides. This version is made with pound cake, which has a firmer texture than sponge. Store-bought pound or sponge cake can also be used.

To make the cake, preheat the oven to 350° F. Butter and flour an 8½ × 4½ inch loaf pan.

In a mixing bowl, cream together the butter and sugar with an electric mixer. Add the boiling water, then beat in the eggs and vanilla until smooth. Set aside. In another bowl, mix together the sifted cake flour, baking powder, and salt, then add to the egg mixture in batches, beating for sev-

CAKE
- ¾ c. (1½ sticks) unsalted butter, softened
- 1 c. sugar
- 3 Tbsp. boiling water
- 4 large eggs
- 2 tsp. vanilla
- 1⅓ c. sifted cake flour
- 1 tsp. baking powder
- ¼ tsp. salt

TRIFLE LAYERS
- ½ c. strawberry preserves (or use any fruit preserves)
- 2 16-oz. cans pear halves, drained (pears can be in syrup or natural juices, or fresh poached pears can also be used)
- ½ c. rum (for a lighter flavor, use sherry)
- 8 oz. semisweet chocolate
- ¾ c. heavy cream

GARNISH
Whipped cream, glacéed cherries or fresh strawberries, slivered almonds, and candied violets (optional)

eral seconds after each addition. Scrape down the sides of the bowl and beat for 1 minute at medium speed, then pour into the prepared pan and smooth the top. Bake 45 to 50 minutes or until a toothpick inserted in the center comes out clean. Cool 10 minutes in the pan, then remove and cool on a rack. Once the cake is completely cool, slice across into $\frac{1}{2}$-inch slices.

To layer the trifle, spread each slice of cake liberally with the preserves and cut into cubes. Set aside. Slice the pear halves lengthwise into 3 or 4 slices and cut in half across. Put the pears in a bowl and pour the rum over them. Let sit for 10 minutes, then drain, reserving the rum. In a large glass trifle bowl (6- to 7-cup capacity) or individual glass bowls, place a layer of jam-covered cake cubes, then layer a portion of pears, alternating with cake, until filled. The top layer should be cake. Pour the remaining rum over all. Set aside.

Next, finely chop the chocolate and place in a bowl. Heat the cream in a small saucepan, almost to a boil, then slowly add the chocolate, stirring until smooth. If the chocolate does not become entirely smooth, push through a fine strainer with a rubber spatula. Pour over the cake, pressing the cake cubes away from the sides of the bowl with a spatula to allow the chocolate to flow down the sides. Cool at room temperature for 15 minutes, then chill in the refrigerator several hours so the flavors intensify. Garnish as desired.

Serves 8

Frozen Pineapple Pudding

This unusually rich pineapple delicacy, which has the added novelty of being a frozen dessert, was described by Mrs. Mary F. Henderson in *Practical Cooking and Dinner Giving* in 1877. A cross between an ice cream and a pudding, it doesn't require an ice-cream maker and can be frozen in your regular freezer. For a traditional presentation, reserve the top of the pineapple and use the leaves to crown the pudding.

8 large eggs, separated
1¼ c. sugar
3 c. heavy cream
¼ tsp. salt
2 c. pineapple puree (1 fresh pineapple, skinned, cut in chunks, and pureed)
2 c. whipped cream (optional)

Combine the egg yolks and sugar in a medium bowl and beat until a yellow ribbon forms when the beater is lifted. Meanwhile, heat the cream until boiling. Dribble the cream into the yolk mixture, beating constantly and taking care not to cook the yolks. Transfer the mixture to a saucepan, add the salt, and cook over medium heat for 5 to 10 minutes, stirring constantly with a whisk until the mixture thickens. Do not allow to boil. Remove from the heat and stir in the pineapple puree. Allow to cool before turning into a covered plastic container and freezing. Serve garnished with pineapple leaves, if desired.

Makes 1½ quarts

Authentic Variation: This version is rich enough without the additional 2 cups of whipped cream that Mrs. Henderson suggests. But if desired, whip and fold into mixture before turning into tubs and freezing.

Makes 2½ quarts

LITTLE PEOPLE HAVE VERY LITTLE FAITH IN SANTA WHO ARRIVES BY ANY OTHER WAY THAN THE CHIMNEY ROUTE.

—1890

Chocolate Chestnut Bavarian

Bavarians—custards combined with cream and flavoring, with gelatin as a setting agent—are not an everyday dessert, but can add special drama to a holiday meal. This one, like a sweet yet sophisticated mousse, combines two of the 19th century's favorite flavors, chestnut and chocolate. It can also be made in individual molds.

1 envelope unflavored gelatin
⅓ c. cold water
4 large egg yolks
1⅓ c. sugar
½ c. milk
1¾ c. heavy cream
1 tsp. vanilla
2 oz. semisweet chocolate, melted
1 oz. sweet (German) chocolate, melted
⅔ c. chestnut puree (¾ c. drained, canned chestnuts will yield this when pureed)
Chocolate sauce to serve (optional)

Combine the gelatin and cold water in a large bowl. Set aside. In medium bowl, whisk the egg yolks and 1 cup of the sugar until light. In a medium saucepan, heat the milk and ½ cup of the heavy cream until bubbles appear around the edges. Do not boil. Very gradually pour the milk mixture over the yolk mixture, whisking continually. Return the mixture to the saucepan and stir continually over medium heat until the mixture coats the back of a spoon, about 5 minutes. Do not allow to boil. Remove from the heat. Pour into the gelatin mixture and whisk until smooth. Add the vanilla and set aside.

Meanwhile, combine both melted chocolates and the chestnut puree, stirring until smooth. Stir this into the gelatin mixture until it is uniformly smooth (it may help to pass the mixture through a strainer, pushing it through with

the back of a rubber spatula). Chill the mixture until thickened, stirring frequently so it does not solidify, about 25 to 35 minutes.

While the chocolate-chestnut mixture is thickening, prepare a mold or molds with at least 4-cup capacity, or a similarly sized bowl, by lightly rinsing with cold water and lightly oiling. Whip the remaining 1¼ cups cream and ⅓ cup sugar in a bowl until stiff and fold into the chocolate mixture. Pour into the mold, smooth the top, and cover with plastic wrap. Refrigerate until solid (about 5 hours or overnight). Unmold by running a knife around the inner edge and dipping the mold briefly into hot water, then turn out onto a plate. Serve ice-cold with chocolate sauce, if desired.

Serves 6 to 8

WHIPPED CREAM IS A DELICATE GARNISH FOR ALL BAVARIAN CREAMS, BLANC-MANGES, FROZEN PUDDINGS AND ICE CREAMS.
—MARIA PARLOA, 1880

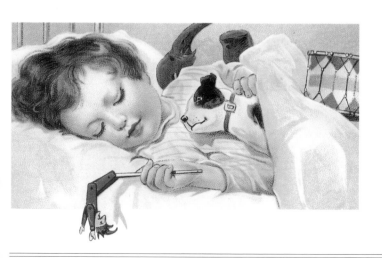

Quince Snow

This refreshing quince snow, made according to a recipe from the 1887 _White House Cookbook,_ is like an apple froth, smooth, mild, and creamy, with bits of quince. It can be garnished with a sprig of fresh rosemary.

3½ c. water
5 quinces, cored and quartered
½ c. sugar
3 large egg whites
Sprig of rosemary to garnish (optional)

Bring 3 cups water to a boil in a large saucepan over high heat. Add the quinces and return to a boil. Reduce the heat to low and simmer 30 to 45 minutes, partially covered, or until the quinces are tender when pierced with a knife. Drain, cool, and when cool enough to handle, peel. Then push the quinces through a coarse sieve.

Meanwhile, in a medium-size saucepan combine the sugar and ½ cup water, and bring to a boil over medium-high heat. Reduce the heat and simmer uncovered 5 to 10 minutes, or until the syrup reaches 235° F. on a candy thermometer. Beat the 3 egg whites until frothy. Continue beating until they form peaks. Carefully beat in the hot syrup and continue beating until all the syrup has been added and the mixture has doubled in volume and is shiny. Add the mashed quince and continue beating until well combined. Place in the freezer to chill until firm but not frozen solid, before serving. Serve in individual glass dishes, with a sprig of fresh rosemary, if desired.

Makes 1½ quarts, or enough for 8 to 12 people

Apricot Velvet in Pastry Baskets

This unusual, very rich dessert, which dates back to 1908, has a creamy, mousselike texture that's soft but firm. For a stronger apricot taste (19th-century apricots were probably more flavorful than ours), use either dried apricots (steamed or boiled) or fresh apricots in season (poach halves in sugar syrup, then puree) instead of canned as specified. Serve in custard cups or in cookielike pastry "baskets."

1 recipe pastry tartlets
(see Morello Cherry Tartlets,
    page 46)
2 17-oz. cans apricot halves,
    drained
6 small to medium egg
    yolks
1 c. sugar
2 c. heavy cream
3 to 4 Tbsp. Maraschino
    liqueur

Prepare the pastry baskets following the recipe for the tartlet shells on pages 46–47. Set aside until ready to fill.

In a food processor, process the drained apricots until pureed (4 cups). Set aside. In the top of a double boiler, combine the egg yolks and sugar and beat until a yellow ribbon falls from the whisk when it is lifted. Stir in the cream and the pureed apricots. Cook in the double boiler over simmering water, stirring constantly, until the eggs begin to thicken and the custard coats the back of a spoon. Remove from the heat and strain through a fine sieve. Whip the mixture until cool, about 5 to 10 minutes. Stir in the Maraschino, then transfer the mixture to an ice-cream maker and freeze according to the manufacturer's directions. Spoon into pastry baskets.

Makes 1½ quarts, or enough for 8 to 10 baskets

Holiday Mint Ice

Many famous cooks created recipes for simple water ices, which were made with water, flavored with fruit juice, and sweetened. When this bright, leafy-green crystalline ice is left to ripen overnight in the freezer, the fresh mint taste can take your breath away. Serve in clear glasses for holiday parties, with a sprig of mint and a candy cane.

1   qt. water
1   c. sugar
½   c. lemon juice
1   tsp. peppermint extract
3   drops green food coloring

In a medium saucepan, bring the water to a boil over medium-high heat. Add the sugar, lemon juice, and peppermint extract (for a milder mint taste, reduce the amount of extract). Remove from the heat and allow to cool. Stir in the green food coloring, then transfer the mixture to an ice-cream maker and freeze according to the manufacturer's directions.

Makes 5 cups

THE SCHOLAR'S TREE

IN MANY SUNDAY SCHOOLS—
AND IT IS A BEAUTIFUL IDEA—A
"SCHOLAR'S TREE" IS PREPARED
ON WHICH THE REGULAR PUPILS
OF THE SCHOOL HANG ONE OR
MORE GIFTS WHICH THEY HAVE
ESPECIALLY CHOSEN AS SUITED
TO CERTAIN POOR CHILDREN
WHOM THEY ARE PRIVILEGED
TO INVITE. A PLEASING ENTER-
TAINMENT, GAMES, AND A GEN-
EROUS SUPPER ARE PROVIDED,
BESIDES A "REAL LIVE SANTA"
WHO PRESIDES OVER THE FES-
TIVITIES AND DISTRIBUTES THE
PRESENTS PERSONALLY.
—MRS. A.G. LEWIS,
DECEMBER 1890

PIES, TARTS, CAKES, AND COOKIES

NEXT TO THE PUDDING, pie once held a place of pride at the end of every Victorian dinner, but especially so on Thanksgiving, when three or four different kinds would have provided a triumphant end to the feast. Pumpkin pie, made from stewed pumpkin, was de rigueur, but all sorts of other pies were served—dried apple pie, berry pies, and small tartlets, as well as creamy custard pies flavored with nutmeg or lemon and covered with meringue or whipped cream. Using the same basic recipe for pie crusts and tart shells, and a variety of sizes, today's cooks can fill a table of trays and pedestals with pies and tarts to bring a flourish to a holiday meal.

Before the modern mania for everything "light" took hold, dark spice and fruit and nut cakes dominated the festive table. Since cake making was time-consuming, this type of dense moist cake was best able to "keep"—consequently several could be made in advance. The liberal use of spices such as cloves, cinnamon, and ginger and ingredients like molasses, rosewater, and orange flower water helped mask the slightly chemical taste of saleratus, an early form of baking soda. For the holidays, most of these cakes would have been frosted with hard white icing and profusely decorated. Today, of course, these fruit and spice cakes can still be made well ahead of time.

Fancifully decorated cookies in all sorts of shapes—angels, hearts, trees, stars, animals—were also an indispensable part of the merrymaking. Whimsically shaped sugar cookies decorated with "lace" icing and glued-on paper "scrap" pictures were often hung on the tree as trinkets and later tucked away as special treasures, while macaroons were popular both before and after the turn of the 19th century. The traditional cookies chosen for this book all make ideal gifts, ideal decorations, and ideal nibbling as well.

ARRANGE AROUND JELLIES OR CREAMS A BORDER OF ANY KIND OF DELICATE GREEN, LIKE SMILAX OR PARSLEY, OR OF ROSE LEAVES, AND DOT IT WITH BRIGHT COLORS—PINKS, GERANIUMS, VERBENAS, OR ROSES. REMEMBER THAT THE GREEN SHOULD BE DARK AND THE FLOWERS BRIGHT. —MARIA PARLOA, 1880

WHO WOULD THINK THAT
THERE NEEDED TO BE PLEA FOR
THE CHRISTMAS WREATH! AND
YET, FROM OVER THE COUNTRY,
THE GRADGRINDS OF CIVILIZATION
ARE OBJECTING TO ITS GLOSSY GREEN
LEAVES AND BRIGHT BERRIES, AND
SAYING THAT IT IS NOTHING BUT A
BIT OF SENTIMENTALITY! WE WANT
A LITTLE MORE SENTIMENTALITY
IN THIS WORLD AND A LITTLE
LESS REALISM.
—*THE LADIES' HOME JOURNAL*,
DECEMBER 1890

Eggnog Pie in Walnut Crust

Considered even more extravagant than a Christmas pudding, an eggnog pie would have been the perfect addition to a New Year's Day buffet. This eggnog filling is similar to the sherry-spiked, nutmeg-sprinkled frozen eggnog described in *Dainty & Artistic Desserts,* a turn-of-the-century cooking pamphlet. Nut crusts, particularly those made from almonds, also feature in Victorian cookery. This tempting holiday pie has a buttery walnut crust and a potent eggnog custard spiked with both brandy and rum. Freshly grated nutmeg boosts the flavor even more.

CRUST
2¼ c. coarsely ground walnuts
⅓ c. sugar
¼ c. (½ stick) unsalted butter, melted
⅛ tsp. ground nutmeg

FILLING
2½ c. heavy cream
1 c. sugar
½ c. brandy
¼ c. rum
1 envelope plus 2 tsp. unflavored gelatin
4 large egg yolks
1 c. milk
¼ tsp. freshly grated nutmeg
Sweetened Whipped Cream to serve (optional; recipe follows)

To make the crust, preheat the oven to 375° F. and set aside a 9-inch pie plate. In a food processor, grind the walnuts with the sugar. Add the melted butter and nutmeg. Mix well and turn into the pie plate. With the back of a spoon or a spatula, press the nut mixture evenly over the bottom and sides of the dish, forming a ½-inch raised edge. Chill for 30 minutes. Bake for 10 minutes or until the edges become brown. Cool to room temperature.

To make the filling, whip 1½ cups heavy cream and ⅔ cup sugar into firm peaks. Set aside in the refrigerator until ready to use. In a small bowl, pour the brandy and rum

together and sprinkle the gelatin over them. Stir and let sit while preparing the custard. Whisk together the egg yolks and the remaining ⅓ cup sugar. Combine the milk and 1 cup of the heavy cream in a saucepan, stirring frequently and heating until small bubbles form around the edge. Add this mixture gradually to the yolks until completely combined, whisking continuously. Pour back into the saucepan and over medium-low heat continuously stir until the mixture coats the back of a spoon (temperature of 172° to 175° F.). Remove from the heat and stir in the rum mixture. Pour into a medium bowl and place in a slightly larger bowl filled with ice. Stir frequently. When the custard mixture starts to set, quickly stir in the refrigerated whipped cream mixture. Pour into the pie shell, smooth the top, and sprinkle with freshly grated nutmeg. Chill 4 to 6 hours. Garnish with Sweetened Whipped Cream, if desired.

Serves 8

IF, WHEN TAKING A CUSTARD PIE OUT OF THE OVEN, IT SHOULD FALL ON THE FLOOR, UPSIDE DOWN, IT IS A SIGN SOMEONE HAS DIED AND LEFT YOU A GREAT FORTUNE.
—*HOME SECRETS*

Sweetened Whipped Cream

In a medium bowl, beat the cream and confectioners' sugar to stiff peaks.

Makes 1 cup

1 c. heavy cream
1½ Tbsp. confectioners' sugar

Dried Apple & Cranberry Pie

Dried fruits, particularly dried apples, a necessary ingredient in the prerefrigeration era, still make an unusual pie that's not only delicious but easy to make. This recipe, made with unsulfured organic dried apples to most closely approximate old-time flavor, has been adapted from several vintage cookbooks, all from the 1880s. Some old-time recipes require dried fruits to be soaked overnight; this one calls for stewing the fruits in a saucepan.

To make the crust, combine the flour and salt in a medium-sized bowl. With a pastry blender or two knives, cut in the butter until crumbly. Dissolve the baking soda in the water. Gradually add the water, and combine until the dough firms. (More water may be required to make a firm dough.) Divide the dough in half, and form two balls, flattening each slightly. Cover the dough with plastic wrap, and chill until ready to use.

Preheat the oven to 400° F. In a large saucepan, stew the dried apples with enough water to cover, over medium heat, until firm but soft (about 20 to 30 minutes). Then drain, reserving ½ cup liquid. Set aside. Combine the sugar, flour, cinnamon, nutmeg, cloves, and lemon and orange

BUTTER CRUST FOR ONE PIE

2⅔ c. flour
    Pinch of salt
½ c. (1 stick) butter, unsalted
6 Tbsp. water
½ tsp. baking soda

FILLING

5 c. dried apples slices (available at health food and specialty stores and some supermarkets, or by mail from The Victorian Cupboard, call 1-800-653-8033)
½ c. sugar (or to taste)
1 Tbsp. flour
¾ tsp. ground cinnamon
¼ tsp. ground nutmeg
¼ tsp. ground clove
½ tsp. grated lemon zest
½ tsp. grated orange zest
½ c. dried cranberries (more if desired)

zests. Add reserved liquid and stir. Combine the mixture with the drained apples, and stir in the cranberries.

Remove the dough from the refrigerator. Roll out each ball onto a lightly floured board with a floured rolling pin. Transfer one dough circle to a 9-inch pie plate. Spread the filling evenly in the pie shell; cover with top crust, and trim and crimp the edges to seal. Cut vents in the top crust. Bake 50 minutes or until lightly golden. Cool on a wire rack.

Serves 8

OUR CHRISTMAS TODAY MAKES ME SOMETIMES FEEL THAT THE CHRISTMAS OF OUR YOUTH IS DEGENERATING INTO A FESTIVAL OF THE STORE-KEEPERS. ONCE THERE WAS MERRY-MAKING AT HOME, TRIMMING THE HOME WITH EVERGREENS, LISTENING FOR THE BELLS OF CHRISTMAS PEALING THROUGH THE FROSTY AIR, AND INTERCHANGE OF GIFTS WHOSE VALUE WAS CHIEFLY IN THEIR HANDIWORK. NOW WE ARE IN DANGER OF ALLOWING CURIOSITY AND ACQUISITIVENESS TO DROWN OUT ALL THE SIMPLE AND SACRED FEELING THAT BELONG TO THE DAY.
—HARRIET PRESCOTT SPOFFORD, 1890

Morello Cherry Tartlets

During the 19th century the word "tart" referred to a large, shallow pie; small individual pies, made in "puff pans" (similar to our cupcake or muffin pans) were known as "tartlets." Festive-looking tartlets like these, filled with fruit, are a pretty sight at holiday time or for a special tea (the liberal use of white sugar once indicated that they weren't for every day). Since cherries are a summer fruit, these were prepared with canned cherries (the Victorians would also have used canned or preserved fruit). The recipe is inspired by an 1861 recipe by Mrs. Isabella Beeton, who suggested adding a few currants for a nice piquant taste.

TART CRUST
3 c. all-purpose flour
1 tsp. salt
10 Tbsp. (1¼ sticks) unsalted butter, cold, cut in small pieces
6 Tbsp. solid vegetable shortening, cold
6 to 8 Tbsp. cold water
⅓ c. cherry jam, melted

FILLING
2¼ c. sour pitted morello cherries, drained if canned or jarred, with syrup reserved (should yield 1⅓ c. light cherry syrup)
2 Tbsp. cornstarch
⅔ c. sugar
4 tsp. lemon juice
½ tsp. almond extract
Sweetened Whipped Cream to serve (optional; see page 43)

To make the crust, combine the flour and salt in a large bowl or food processor. Cut in the butter and shortening with a pastry blender or two knives, until the mixture resembles crumbs. Add the water 1 tablespoon at a time, mixing well or processing until the dough holds its shape. Separate into halves, flatten into disks, then wrap with plastic wrap and refrigerate for 30 minutes. Cut each half into 4 pieces. Shape each piece into a small ball and roll out into a 6-inch circle on a lightly floured board. Place each crust in a 4½-inch tart pan (there will be an overlap of ¼ to ½ inch). Fold in and level the edge, smoothing dough on the bottom and sides to $\frac{1}{4}$-inch thickness. Prick several times on the bottom with a fork, and refrigerate the shells for 30 minutes.

Preheat the oven to 425° F. Line each tart crust with wax paper or foil and fill with beans, rice, or pie weights. Bake for 10 minutes, remove from the oven, then remove the pie weights and paper or foil and brush the shells with the melted cherry jam. Return the tartlets to the oven and bake an additional 10 minutes, watching carefully so they don't become too brown (the edges should be golden or light brown). Remove from the oven and cool on a rack.

To make the filling, in a small bowl, stir 3 tablespoons of the cherry syrup into the cornstarch. Set aside. Pour the rest of the syrup into a small saucepan and add the sugar and lemon juice. Bring to a boil, stirring to dissolve the sugar. Add the syrup mixture and stir till thickened, about 1 minute. Remove from the heat, add the almond extract, and let cool slightly. Divide the cherries equally among the tartlet shells and spoon the thickened syrup mixture over each one. Let set at room temperature. Remove tart shells from the pan and serve.

Serves 8

Father Christmas Iced Spice & Nut Cake

The culinary roots of this rich and gingery cake, adapted from several 19th-century recipes, go back many generations. Decorate by drizzling with the traditional hard white icing and a sprig of holly (but don't eat or cook the holly—it's poisonous). It also makes a lovely gift, wrapped in cellophane and tied with a colorful bow. For a quaint old-fashioned flavor, try adding a teaspoon of rosewater to the icing. Prior to the widespread availability of vanilla flavoring, rosewater was a common substitute. Orange flower water, another old-time flavoring, can also be used.

Toast the almonds by placing in a dry skillet or frying pan over medium heat, stirring frequently. When lightly browned, remove from the heat. Set aside.

Preheat the oven to 350° F. Butter and flour a 10-inch bundt pan. In a medium bowl, combine the cake flour, baking powder, baking soda, salt, and spices. In a large mixing bowl or the bowl of an electric mixer, cream the butter and sugar until light, then add the molasses and combine well. Add the eggs one at a time, beating well after each addition. Add the vanilla. Add the dry ingredients gradually. Beat on medium speed for 1 minute. Fold in the walnuts and raisins

CAKE

1 c. toasted almonds
3½ c. sifted cake flour
2 tsp. baking powder
½ tsp. baking soda
½ tsp. salt
2 tsp. ground cinnamon
2 tsp. ground ginger
1 tsp. ground nutmeg
½ tsp. cloves
½ tsp. mace
1¼ c. (2 ½ sticks) unsalted
butter, softened
1¼ c. sugar
⅔ c. molasses
4 large eggs
1¼ tsp. vanilla
1 c. chopped walnuts
1 c. golden raisins

ICING

1 Tbsp. plus 1 tsp. milk
(plus more if needed)
1½ tsp. vanilla (or rosewater
or orange flower water)
1 c. confectioners' sugar

and almonds and pour into the prepared pan. Bake 45 minutes or until a toothpick inserted in the middle comes out clean. Cool 10 to 15 minutes on a rack, then invert the cake onto the rack to cool completely.

To make the icing, stir together the milk, vanilla, and confectioners' sugar until smooth. If it seems stiff, add up to 1 tablespoon additional milk. Spoon over the cake, letting some of it drizzle down the sides in a decorative manner.

Serves 8

Twelfth Night Cake

The period from Christmas to Twelfth Night or "Little Christmas" (the eve of January 5) was the time when children's holiday parties were traditionally held, culminating on the twelfth night, which commemorated the arrival of the Wise Men in Bethlehem, with a gala party during which a Twelfth Night Cake was served. A typical cake was enormous and frosted with hard white icing and ornamented with fondants, holly sprays, or fancy sugar and gum figures. According to tradition, a dry bean should be baked in the batter of the cake. Whichever gentleman found the bean in his portion became "king" of the evening's festivities. If it was found by a lady, she had the honor of providing the cake for the following year. This recipe has been adapted to serve eight.

Preheat the oven to 375° F. Butter an 8½-inch springform pan. Line the pan with a piece of wax paper cut to size, then buttered and floured. Set aside.

In a small bowl, combine the flour, salt, and baking powder. In a large mixing bowl or the bowl of an electric mixer, cream the butter, then add the sugar and egg yolks and beat well. Stir in the brandy, almond extract, orange

CAKE

2 c. sifted cake flour
¼ tsp. salt
¾ tsp. baking powder
½ c. (1 stick) unsalted butter, softened
¾ c. sugar
3 large eggs, separated
2 tsp. brandy
½ tsp. almond extract
2 Tbsp. finely chopped candied orange rind (see recipe, page 68, or available at confectionery and specialty stores and some supermarkets)
2 Tbsp. finely chopped dried apricots
1 c. blanched almonds, chopped coarsely and toasted (to toast, see directions on page 48)
1 dry bean

GLAZE

⅓ c. confectioners' sugar
1 tsp. orange juice
1 tsp. lemon juice

rind, and apricots. Add the flour mixture and stir to combine. Mix together on low speed. Stir in the almonds.

In another bowl, beat the egg whites until stiff but not dry peaks form, then fold into the batter. Place the dry bean in the prepared pan, and pour in the batter. Bake for 25 to 30 minutes, until the top is golden and a toothpick inserted in the center comes out clean. Cool on a rack for 5 to 10 minutes. Run a knife around the edge and remove the sides of the pan. Invert the cake and remove the bottom and wax paper. Cool completely.

To make the glaze, mix the confectioners' sugar with the orange and lemon juices. Spoon on the cake; garnish as desired.

Serves 8

St. Nick's prowling
around in the snow.
While you're smuggling
comfy and all aglow,
He's headed straight
for your own house.
And in he'll steal
as quiet as a
mouse.

CHRISTMAS

White Wine Fruitcake

Glistening with golden pineapple, crimson cherries, and other glacéed fruits, a fine fruitcake mellowing in the cupboard is a perennial holiday treat. This cake is a lightened version of the traditional favorite, adapted from an 1880s recipe by Miss Parloa. Made with white wine instead of brandy, it offers a change from the typical dark loaf we associate with 19th-century holidays, and may convert even those skeptics who normally eschew fruitcake altogether. Any combination of your favorite fruits and nuts can be substituted for those in here. The cake can be made up to a month in advance.

Preheat the oven to 325° F. Butter and flour an 8¼ × 4½ inch loaf pan. In a medium bowl, mix the flour, baking powder, salt, allspice, and cinnamon. In another bowl, mix the candied orange rind, candied pineapple, pears, raisins, apple, and almonds with the wine. In a large mixing bowl or the bowl of an electric mixer, beat the butter and sugar until light. Add the eggs one at a time, beating well after each addition. Add the flour mixture and milk, alternating the two, until fully combined. Mix on medium-high speed for 1 minute. Fold in the fruit mixture, and add coconut, if desired. Spread in the prepared pan. Smooth the top and bake for 50 to 55 minutes, or until a toothpick inserted in the

1½ c. all-purpose flour
1 tsp. baking powder
½ tsp. salt
½ tsp. allspice
¼ tsp. cinnamon
⅔ c. finely chopped candied orange rind (see recipe, page 68, or available at confectionery and specialty stores and some supermarkets)
⅔ c. candied pineapple, chopped (see above)
⅔ c. finely chopped dried pears
⅓ c. golden raisins
¼ c. finely chopped dried apple
¼ c. finely chopped blanched almonds
½ c. sweet white wine (such as muscatel)
10 Tbsp. (1¼ sticks) unsalted butter, softened
¾ c. sugar
2 large eggs
¼ c. milk
½ c. grated coconut (optional, but in many 19th-century recipes)

center comes out clean. Cool for 5 minutes in the pan, then turn out onto a wire rack to cool completely. The cake can be eaten once it is cool, or wrapped in wine-soaked cheese-cloth, refrigerated, and brushed from time to time with more wine to keep the cloth moist. If refrigerated, it should be tightly wrapped in foil over the cheesecloth.

Serves 8

MANY OF THE OLD-FASHIONED BUT EXCELLENT RECEIPTS FOR CAKE CONTAIN WINE OR BRANDY. I HAVE GIVEN THEM AS THEY HAVE BEEN HANDED DOWN TO ME, AND CAN VOUCH FOR THEIR QUALITY. THE AMOUNT OF LIQUOR USED IS SO SMALL AS TO GIVE NO DECIDED FLAVOR. INDEED, ITS PRESENCE WOULD NEVER BE SUSPECTED.
—MRS. MARY B. WELCH, 1884

Caramel-Glazed Chocolate Nougat Cake

After the 1860s, with the advent of baking powder, cake making became easier. These new cakes, lighter and fluffier than the older fruited pound cakes, had a fashionable flair which appealed to the Victorian sense of novelty. At about the same time, chocolate became a Victorian favorite. A chocolate cake like this one, made with mashed potatoes for additional moistness and adapted from *Dozens of Good Things,* a 1915 cookbook, would have been suitable for any special occasion.

To make the cake, preheat the oven to 375° F. Butter the bottom of an 8½-inch springform pan. Line with wax paper cut to fit inside, buttered and floured. Set aside.

On a piece of wax paper, roll out the almond paste to form an 8-inch circle. Set aside. In a medium bowl, mix the flour, baking powder, baking soda, salt, cinnamon, mace, and cloves. Set aside. In a large mixing bowl, beat the butter until light and add the sugar. Beat well. Add the eggs and beat until thoroughly combined. Add the mashed potato and beat until the mixture looks lightly curdled. Add the melted chocolate and almond extract. Alternately add the dry ingredients and milk until combined. Beat for 1 minute on medium speed. Stir in the chopped nuts. Pour half of the

CAKE
- 1 8-oz. can almond paste
- 1¾ c. sifted cake flour
- 1½ tsp. baking powder
- ½ tsp. baking soda
- ¼ tsp. salt
- ½ tsp. ground cinnamon
- ½ tsp. ground mace
- ⅛ tsp. ground cloves
- ½ c. (1 stick) unsalted butter, softened
- 1 c. sugar
- 2 large eggs
- ½ c. mashed potato
- 1½ oz. semisweet chocolate, melted
- 1 tsp. almond extract
- ½ c. milk
- 1 c. finely chopped natural (not blanched) almonds

GLAZE
- 4 Tbsp. unsalted butter
- ⅔ c. brown sugar, packed
- 1½ Tbsp. heavy cream
- ¼ tsp. almond extract
- ½ c. toasted slivered almonds (to toast, see directions on page 48)

mixture into the prepared pan and smooth the top. Place the circle of almond paste on top, then pour in the remaining batter. Bake for 45 to 50 minutes or until a toothpick inserted in the center comes out clean. Cool in the pan on a wire rack for 15 minutes, then remove the sides and cool completely. Remove the pan bottom and wax paper before glazing.

To make the glaze, stir together the butter, sugar, and cream in a saucepan. Heat on medium heat until well blended, then bring to a boil over medium-high heat. Remove from the heat and add the almond extract. Pour over the cake, tilting it from side to side so the glaze spreads evenly. Top with the slivered almonds. Cool 8 to 10 minutes until the glaze is set.

A CAKE CONTAINING BUTTER WILL KEEP A WEEK IN A TIGHT CAKE BOX.—1883

Serves 10

Lemon Almond Jumbles

Recipes for these nostalgic little sugar cookies can be found in the earliest 19th-century cookbooks. This variation, which combines two popular flavors, can be rolled in slivered almonds as directed, or cut into shapes and decorated for Christmas and New Year's with colored frosting. Ideal for a Christmas tea, trays of these delicately flavored jumbles are also a nice treat on a cold winter night, served with mulled cider. They can be made up to a month in advance and frozen till ready to use.

1 c. (2 sticks) unsalted butter, softened
¾ c. plus 1 Tbsp. sugar
1 large egg
1½ tsp. almond extract
5 tsp. grated lemon zest (more or less if desired)
2 Tbsp. lemon juice
2 c. all-purpose flour
¼ tsp. salt
⅔ c. blanched, chopped toasted almonds (to toast, see directions on page 48)

Cream the butter and ¾ cup of the sugar until light and fluffy. Add the egg, almond extract, and lemon zest and juice, and mix well. Gradually beat in the flour and salt to form a dough. Wrap in plastic wrap and chill for 10 to 15 minutes so the dough will be easier to handle, then separate into two portions. Roll each into a cylinder 8½ inches long by 1¼ inches in diameter. Wrap the cylinder separately and chill 8 to 10 minutes.

Take two pieces of plastic wrap, sprinkle half of the almonds on each, and half the remaining tablespoon of sugar, mixing them well. Roll each dough cylinder in the mix, distributing it equally over the dough. Rewrap the

ANOTHER PRETTY (AND GOOD) LITTLE CAKE IS TO MAKE A BATCH OF JUMBLES, BAKED VERY THIN AND STICK THEM, SMOOTH SIDE TOGETHER WITH CHOCOLATE FROSTING.
—*THE LADIES' WORLD*, 1902

cylinders and refrigerate for 1 hour until firm.

Preheat the oven to 350° F. Slice the rolls into $\frac{1}{4}$-inch slices and place the slices $\frac{3}{4}$ inch apart on an ungreased cookie sheet. Bake 10 to 12 minutes, until lightly browned. Cool on a rack.

Makes 5 dozen jumbles

MARKING COOKIES IN GOLD

BAKE ROUND CAKES FOR THE CHILDREN AND WHEN THE FROSTING ON THEM IS HARD, DIP A SMALL BRUSH INTO THE YOLK OF AN EGG, AND WRITE A WORD OR NAME UPON THE CAKES. IT PLEASES THE LITTLE ONES VERY MUCH.

—MARIA PARLOA, 1880

Gingerbread Men, Hearts, and Drops

More than any other cookie, gingerbread is associated with the Christmas season. Its fragrant dough can be fashioned into simple shapes to hang on a tree, or sturdy men decorated with traditional icing, currants, and buttons, as well as spicy cookies for dessert.

This "triple ginger" recipe (it features ground ginger, ginger juice, and crystallized ginger) produces an exceptional gingerbread with a soft, cakelike texture. It can be spooned into puffy little drops, rolled into flattened hearts, or made into old-fashioned gingerbread men. For a special holiday gift giving, place gingerbread cookies in a keepsake box or decorative tin lined with old-fashioned paper lace, and tie with a big bow.

2½ c. all-purpose flour
¾ tsp. baking soda
½ tsp. salt
¾ tsp. ground allspice
¾ tsp. ground ginger
½ c. (1 stick) unsalted butter, softened
⅓ c. sugar, plus extra if making drops
1 large egg
⅓ c. molasses
1 tsp. fresh ginger juice (can be obtained from 2 oz. freshly grated or pureed ginger squeezed by hand)
3 Tbsp. minced crystallized ginger
4 Tbsp. minced dried cherries

Stir the flour, baking soda, salt, allspice, and ground ginger in a medium bowl. Set aside. In a large bowl, beat together the butter and sugar until light. Add the egg, molasses, and ginger juice and beat well. Add the flour mixture in batches and beat to incorporate after each addition. Stir in the crystallized ginger and cherries. Cover the bowl with plastic wrap and chill 1 to 2 hours, or until the dough is easy to handle and roll out.

GINGERBREAD SHOULD ALWAYS BE BAKED WITH A VERY MODERATE FIRE, AS IT IS SO APT TO SCORCH.
—MRS. T.J. KIRKPATRICK, 1883

Preheat the oven to 375° F. For cutout hearts or ginger-bread men, roll the dough out to ⅛-inch thickness on a lightly floured surface, and cut the cookies with a lightly floured heart-shaped or figure-shaped cookie cutter. For drops, pinch off grape-size pieces, roll them into balls, and roll again in additional sugar. Place the hearts, drops, or gin-gerbread men on a lightly greased cookie sheet and bake 10 minutes. Balls will have a slightly puffed appearance; hearts and men will appear slightly flattened.

Makes 4 dozen drops; yield of hearts and men will vary

BY 1880, FLATTENED GINGERBREAD CAKES WERE OFTEN DECORATED WITH COLORFUL SCRAP PICTURES, WHICH WERE PASTED ON WITH EGG WHITES, AND HUNG BY RIBBONS TO THE TREE.

Balmoral Tartan Shortbread Cookies

A traditional Scottish treat, shortbread is just as traditional in this country, especially at Christmastime. The soft, somewhat crumbly shortbread dough can be pressed into a decorated shortbread mold, rolled into a circle and cut into traditional pie-shaped wedges, or made into Christmas cookies. Cut into rectangles, these Balmoral Tartan cookies are crisscrossed with red and green icing stripes to form a tartan pattern, in a salute to the country home of Queen Victoria. For a slightly chewier, coarser texture, granulated sugar can be substituted for confectioners'.

10 Tbsp. (1¼ sticks)
    unsalted butter, softened
¾ c. confectioners' sugar,
    sifted
1¼ c. all-purpose flour
    Pinch of salt
    Icing (see recipe, page 48)
2 to 3 drops red food
    coloring
2 to 3 drops green food
    coloring

Preheat the oven to 350° F. In a mixing bowl, beat the butter until light. Gradually add the sugar and beat until fully combined. Slowly add the flour and salt and beat until fully combined.

    Roll out the dough between two sheets of wax paper to a 9½-inch square about ¼-inch thick (see Note). Peel off the top paper and invert the dough onto an ungreased baking sheet (it may be easier to put the baking sheet onto the shortbread dough with one hand underneath the dough, then invert so the paper side is up, and peel the paper off). Score the dough with a fork into quarters and score each quarter in sixths. Bake in the oven for 18 to 20 minutes, or

until light brown. Remove from the oven and immediately cut along the score lines. Let the pieces cool for 2 minutes on the pan, then remove to a rack to cool completely.

To decorate, make the icing and divide into two bowls. Mix 2 to 3 drops of red food coloring into one bowl and 2 to 3 drops of green food coloring into the other bowl. Spoon the icing into small plastic bags and seal. With a scissors, snip off a tiny corner of each bag. Squeezing the icing from the bag, draw horizontal green lines across all the cookies. Let set 5 to 10 minutes until dry. Then crisscross with red icing stripes in the opposite direction to form the tartan pattern. Let dry 5 to 10 minutes.

Makes 24 2½ × 1¼ inch cookies

NOTE: If the dough is too warm to roll out due to oversoftening or a warm kitchen, cover with plastic wrap and set in the refrigerator for a few minutes to firm.

Mint Sea-Foam Cookies

An elegant addition to a New Year's Eve brunch or tea, these wonderfully airy meringue confections, inspired by an 1883 recipe from the *Housekeeper's New Cook Book* by Mrs. T.J. Kirkpatrick, are tufted into peaks like bits of foam, and flavored with mint. Sometimes called "kisses," they are a cross between a cookie and a candy, and would look elegant piled in a silver pastry tier or stacked in a holiday pyramid. For a pale-green tint, add a drop of green food coloring to the mixture.

4 large egg whites
¼ tsp. cream of tartar
1 c. sugar, sifted
¾ tsp. peppermint extract

Preheat the oven to 225° F. Line two baking sheets with parchment paper. Set aside. In a large bowl, beat the egg whites until foamy. Add the cream of tartar. Continue beating and slowly add the sugar. Just before the mixture forms stiff peaks, add the peppermint extract. Continue to beat until stiff peaks form. Scoop out heaping tablespoons of batter and set on the parchment 1 inch apart, forming peaks or waves on top of each cookie. Bake for 1 hour. Turn off the oven, but leave the baking sheets in the oven, with the door slightly ajar, for several hours or overnight. Remove the cookies from the parchment before serving.

Makes 3 dozen 2-inch cookies

NOTE: Meringue cannot be successfully made on a humid or rainy day.

NOTHING IS MORE CLOSELY ASSOCIATED WITH A JOYFUL CHRISTMAS-TIDE THAN THE WELL-LADEN TABLE AT DINNER TIME.—1890

MAKE YOUR HOLIDAY TABLES
AS BRIGHT AND CHEERFUL AS
YOU CAN. DO WHAT YOUR
MEANS WILL ALLOW BUT NO
MORE; AND DO NOT I PRAY YOU
OVERWORK YOURSELF SO THAT
THE HOLIDAY SEASON IS MADE A
DRUDGE; INSTEAD OF AS IT
SHOULD BE, THE GLADDEST
TIME OF THE YEAR.
—*MOTHER'S CORNER*, 1890

Merry Christmas

SWEETMEATS, CONFECTIONS, AND FESTIVE PUNCHES

YIELDING TO THE URGE for sinful sweets was much the same in the 19th century as it is today. Thus no holiday celebration was complete without its assortment of fancy bonbons, old-fashioned peppermints, homey molasses, and other homemade candies.

Some of these confections—like spiced nuts, candied citrus peel, and old-fashioned popcorn balls—need little introduction and are disarmingly simple to make. And while candy making does require some skill, we have the advantage over our great-great-grandmothers of the candy thermometer, which lets us know the precise moment when boiling is sufficient to produce a hard or soft result. Although it may take time and patience to make the perfect confection, once you do, you'll have delectable homemade sweetmeats for everyone on your Christmas list, as well as to share when family and friends come to visit.

Christmas dinner was always preceded by glasses of champagne, punch, or wine, which continued to be served throughout the meal. Afterward, more punch, cordials, mulled wine, or eggnog was brought forth. During the 19th century, punch referred to a sweet, hot or cold, lightly alcoholic or nonalcoholic fruit juice–based drink (the types of fruit juices used depended on the season and flavor one wished to emphasize). The basic formula was citrus juice and water, along with sugar, spices, and brandy, rum, wine, sherry, or champagne, served in a punch bowl over an 8- to 10-pound block of ice. Often a recipe called for the punch to be slightly frozen, then left to ripen before serving.

The punches and bowls here not only are guaranteed to lend a little authentic sparkle to the holiday season, but are suitable for special occasions all year round.

HAND-LETTERED MENU CARDS SET IN DAINTY HOLDERS HELPED SET THE STAGE FOR A MEMORABLE EVENING. TODAY THEY CAN BE USED TRADITIONALLY— AT EVERY PLACE SETTING—OR AT EITHER END OF THE DINING TABLE.

Port & Spice Glazed Nuts

For centuries, spiced and sugared nuts—almonds, walnuts, filberts, hazelnuts, and pecans—were doused in white and brown sugar (or even sugar tinted pink) and baked into one of the season's easiest treats. This irresistible recipe shows off nuts at their sweetest, soaked in port (the favorite of 19th-century gentlemen), then lavishly rolled in sugar and savory spices, and baked.

2 large egg whites
4 Tbsp. port (or brandy, sherry, or champagne)
1⅓ c. pecan halves
1⅓ c. whole natural (not blanched) almonds
1⅓ c. walnut halves
1⅓ c. sugar
2 tsp. salt
1 tsp. ground cinnamon
1 tsp. ground cardamom
1 tsp. ground ginger
1 tsp. ground allspice

Preheat the oven to 275°F. Lightly grease two large baking sheets or a jelly roll pan. In a mixing bowl, beat the egg whites until slightly frothy. Add the port. Add the nuts, stirring until they are well distributed and evenly covered. Set aside. In another bowl, mix together the sugar, salt, and spices. Separate into two small bowls (see Note). Taking a small spoonful at a time, drop the nuts into the sugar-and-spice mixture and coat thoroughly, using up the first bowl before beginning the second. Place in a single layer on the prepared baking sheet. Bake for 1 hour.

Makes 4 cups

NOTE: If all the sugar-and-spice mixture is placed in one bowl, it will become too wet from the port.

Candied Lemon and Orange Rind

Candied lemon and orange rinds, a kind of sugarplum, can be made many months in advance of the holidays and packed away in canisters until ready to be used. They are excellent as a holiday gift (fill a big old-fashioned glass jar and tie with a silk cord and tassel), baked in a fruitcake, or presented as glittering and tasty after-dinner sweetmeats, in a silver or cut-glass serving dish.

2½ c. sugar, plus extra to coat the rinds
1 qt. water
Rind of 2 oranges and 2 lemons, cut into strips

Make a syrup by bringing the sugar and water to a boil in a saucepan over medium heat. Lower the heat and simmer gently, then drop the strips of rind into the syrup and cook for about 1 hour or until the rinds are soft. Remove the rind from the syrup, drain, then roll in additional sugar. Let dry and store in a cool, dry place.

Makes about 1 cup

Traditional Popcorn Balls

Americans have celebrated with popcorn ever since the Indians showed early settlers how to dry corn and roast it until it pops. Today's popcorn is still indispensable for a traditional Yuletide, strung into garlands for the tree or mantel or pinned, kernel by kernel, onto the ends of branches with straight pins.

These sticky syrup-covered balls can be tied with colorful ribbons and used as tree decorations, as party favors, and, of course, for munching. At least two cooks should participate, one to pour the hot syrup, the other to roll the popcorn balls.

2 qt. popped popcorn
1 c. sugar
3 Tbsp. water
1 Tbsp. unsalted butter

Place the popped corn in a large, lightly buttered bowl. Set aside. Combine the sugar, water, and butter in a small heavy saucepan and bring to a boil over medium heat. Boil without stirring until it reaches the "hard ball" stage, when a spoonful dropped into cold water forms a hard ball which holds its shape, yet remains malleable (on a candy thermometer, 260° F.). Pour the syrup over the popped corn, stirring so it is uniformly covered. With lightly buttered hands, quickly mold the syrup-covered corn into balls, pressing hard so the popped kernels adhere. Set the balls aside to dry and harden. The syrup is *hot,* so be careful.

Makes 12 balls, 3 inches in diameter

A LITTLE RED SUGAR CAN BE ADDED TO THE SYRUP IF MORE FANCY LOOKING BALLS ARE DESIRED.
—DR. MILES, PURVEYOR OF DR. MILES RESTORATIVE REMEDIES

Old-Fashioned Molasses Ribbon Twists

Molasses, which once came in barrels from sugar plantations in the South, was the least expensive sweetener and a common substitute for sugar. It lent its distinctive flavor—and strong colonial associations—to many old-fashioned treats, most notably to gingerbread, but it also was a much-beloved old-fashioned candy. This authentic recipe, which produces rich, golden, and buttery molasses ribbon twists, is from *Dr. Price's Delicious Desserts,* a 1904 recipe pamphlet. Although a challenge, it's fun to try with friends in an old-fashioned taffy-pulling party—and the delicious results are well worth it.

1 c. molasses
1 c. sugar
1 Tbsp. unsalted butter
1 Tbsp. white distilled
    vinegar
1 tsp. baking soda

Butter two 8 × 8 inch baking pans and set aside. Combine the molasses, sugar, butter, and vinegar in a heavy-bottomed 3-quart saucepan over medium heat. Stir just until the mixture comes to a boil, occasionally washing down the sides of the pan with a wet brush. Without stirring, boil the mixture until an inserted candy thermometer reaches 270° F. If the mixture seems likely to boil over, again wash down the sides of the pan with the damp brush. At 270° F., take the pan off the heat and stir in the baking soda, continually stirring, which allows the mixture to rise, fall, and become opaque

CANDY-MAKING IS A PLEASANT PASTIME THAT SERVES TO OCCUPY THE ATTENTION OF THE YOUNG AT TIMES WHEN OTHER PURSUITS, FAR MORE DANGEROUS, MIGHT BE INDULGED IN.
—DR. MILES CANDY BOOK

and satiny. This should take several minutes, while you continue to stir. Then pour into the prepared pans, dividing equally. Let cool until it can be handled comfortably. With buttered hands, pull the candy into satiny ropes, bringing the ends in back to the middle and pulling again. Continue pulling until the candy cannot be pulled anymore—about 4 minutes. Twist into $\frac{1}{2}$-inch-thick ropes, then, using buttered scissors, cut into 1-inch pieces. (The candy can also be cut into long molasses "candy canes.") Set the pieces on wax paper, then wrap each piece individually in wax paper and keep in an airtight container, in a cool, dry place.

Makes 6 to $6\frac{1}{2}$ dozen 1-inch-long candies (about 3 pounds)

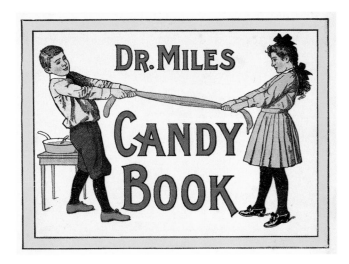

Chocolate Rum Truffles

Introduced to America at the beginning of the 19th century, these meltingly rich and fragrant balls of rum, chocolate, and cream are still guaranteed to elicit sighs of delight from one's guests, especially when passed around on polished silver trays. This recipe was adapted from several vintage recipes for chocolate and rum truffles. A small chunk of crystallized ginger may be place inside each one, if desired. Early recipes also suggest rolling the balls in powdered cocoa to keep them from melting—a nice touch.

To make the centers, chop the chocolate coarsely and place in a food processor. Process until finely chopped and leave in the processor. Heat the cream in small covered saucepan over medium heat until it boils, then immediately pour the cream over the chocolate and process until smooth. Add the butter and continue to process, checking to see if the mixture is totally smooth and glossy. Add the rum and process 10 to 15 seconds more. Scoop the mixture into a small baking pan ($8\frac{1}{2} \times 4\frac{1}{2}$ inches) to a depth of 1 inch and set in the refrigerator to chill for 1 hour or until easy to scoop out with a melon baller. If desired, insert a small piece of crystallized ginger, an almond, or a piece of candied orange or lemon

CENTERS

½ lb. high-quality semisweet chocolate

½ c. heavy cream

2 Tbsp. (¼ stick) unsalted butter, softened

3 Tbsp. rum, at room temperature

Chopped crystallized ginger (optional; available in specialty stores), natural (unblanched) almonds, or candied orange or lemon rind (see recipe, page 68, or available at confectionery and specialty stores and some supermarkets)

COATING

½ lb. high-quality semisweet chocolate

2 Tbsp. (¼ stick) unsalted butter, clarified

Powdered cocoa to coat exterior (optional)

rind in the center of each ball. Place the balls on a wax paper–covered dish in the refrigerator to chill while continuing to scoop. Chill the balls 30 to 45 minutes more. If they are slightly irregular in shape, roll them in your hands quickly to make them rounder before chilling.

To coat the truffles, cover a large plate with wax paper and set aside. Fill a large bowl with cold water and set aside. Chop the chocolate coarsely and place it in the food processor. Process until finely chopped, then pour into the top of a double boiler over barely simmering water. Add the clarified butter and slowly allow the chocolate to melt, stirring constantly and making sure the temperature does not exceed 120° F. Remove the mixture from the heat before it gets to 120° F. or even near it (118° F. or so). Cool the mixture to just below 88° F. by plunging the bottom of the saucepan into a bowl of cold water, making sure no water comes into contact with the chocolate. Then, dip the chilled centers by dropping them into the mixture by hand, lifting them out, shaking off any excess coating, and placing them on a wax paper–covered plate. Put back in the refrigerator for 15 to 20 minutes, then roll them in the powdered cocoa, if desired. Keep the truffles in the refrigerator until ready to serve.

Makes 3 dozen ¾-inch-diameter truffles

GO OUT ONE DOOR AND IN ANOTHER AND YOU SURELY WILL HAVE COMPANY.
—HOME SECRETS

Horehound "Broken Glass" Candy

Horehound is an herb that was used to make candy during the 18th and 19th centuries. Typically a "country store" or "penny" candy, it has a rich, tangy taste and was often used as a remedy for sore throats. This recipe, not as strong-tasting as some horehound, is based on several sources from the 1870s. Not easy to make—this is for experienced candy makers—it resembles beautiful broken pieces of amber-colored glass.

½ oz. dry rubbed horehound (available at health food and specialty stores)
1 c. plus 2 Tbsp. water
6 oz. light brown sugar
6 oz. granulated sugar
¼ tsp. cream of tartar

Bring the dry rubbed horehound and 1 cup water to a boil in a small saucepan, then set aside for 15 minutes to cool. Line a strainer with a double layer of cheesecloth. Suspend the strainer over a bowl and pour the horehound liquid through it. This should yield about ¾ cup horehound water. Set aside ¼ cup for the recipe. Cover and refrigerate the remainder for later use.

Butter a 7 × 11 inch pan and set aside. Put the horehound liquid, brown sugar, white sugar, cream of tartar, and 2 tablespoons of water in a heavy-bottomed 3-quart saucepan. Bring the mixture to a boil over medium heat, stirring constantly. Stop stirring when the mixture reaches a boil, and wash down the sides of the pan with a wet brush. Continue boiling until an inserted candy thermometer

reaches 265° to 270° F. (if the mixture seems likely to boil over, wash down the sides of the pan until the boiling slightly subsides). Pour into the prepared pan and check frequently to see how quickly the mixture is hardening (about 5 to 7 minutes). When it is just hard, pry it out of the pan and place it on a cutting board. Use a large knife to cut into irregular pieces resembling broken glass. Store in an airtight container.

Makes a 7 × 11 inch pan of ⅛-inch-thick pieces

Turkish Jelly Squares

The Victorians called this delicious and unusual sweetmeat "Turkish paste," but it is actually a dainty citrus-flavored jelly candy, rolled in confectioners' sugar and studded with pistachio nuts.

⅔ oz. sheet gelatin (available at specialty stores and some supermarkets)
2½ c. sugar
1 c. water
¼ c. freshly squeezed orange juice
1 Tbsp. freshly squeezed lemon juice
¼ tsp. orange extract
½ c. coarsely chopped pistachios
1½ to 2 c. confectioners' sugar for rolling and coating

Lightly butter an 8 × 8 inch baking pan and set aside. Soak the gelatin in a shallow bowl of cold water. Set aside. Combine the sugar and water in a heavy-bottomed 3-quart saucepan. Stirring to dissolve the sugar, bring the mixture to a boil over medium heat. Once the mixture boils, squeeze the cold water out of the gelatin and add it, stirring slightly, to dissolve. If the mixture starts to boil up, wash down the sides of the pan with a wet brush. Boil for 10 minutes, remove from the heat, and add the orange and lemon juices and orange extract. Stir slightly to combine. Pour into the prepared pan and sprinkle the nuts over the top. Set aside to cool and jell, about 2 hours. When the mixture has completely jelled, cut into 1-inch squares (run the knife around the perimeter of the pan as well). With a fork or spatula, scoop the squares from the pan one at a time and roll in confectioners' sugar. Place the coated pieces in an airtight container with a light layer of confectioners' sugar on the bottom and top. Set aside for at least 2 days. Shake off excess sugar.

Makes 64 1-inch squares

Country Wassail Bowl

Of all the ways to lift one's spirits, none works as well as this richly spiced and potent punch traditionally made from ale, wine, or cider. Wassail (the word means "good health") is served in a large cup or bowl, which is passed around the table. It is particularly popular on New Year's Day, for a traditional Victorian open house.

Preheat the oven to 350° F. Core and peel the apples, then fill with the brown sugar, distributing it evenly among the apples. Place the sugar-filled apples in a baking dish and bake 25 to 30 minutes or until tender. Set aside. In a large saucepan, combine the cider, ginger, cloves, cinnamon, nutmeg, and allspice. Simmer for 10 to 12 minutes, then pour in the sherry and ale. Continue to simmer (do not bring to a boil), and gradually stir in the extra-fine sugar until thoroughly dissolved. Strain the mixture and return to the pan. Add the brandy and lemon or orange rind. Place the apples in the bottom of a large punch bowl and pour in the punch.

Serves 20

6 baking apples
3 c. light brown sugar
1 qt. apple cider
3 tsp. ground ginger
1 Tbsp. whole cloves
2 sticks cinnamon
½ tsp. ground nutmeg
1 Tbsp. whole allspice
2 bottles sherry
2 qt. ale or dark beer
2½ c. extra-fine sugar (available in most supermarkets)
1 c. brandy
½ c. sliced lemon or orange rind

Champagne Bowl with Fresh Raspberries

Champagne provided a proper note of exuberance to Victorian holidays, as it does to our celebrations today (in 1893 *The Art of Entertaining* recommended a champagne bowl similar to this one, served over cracked ice). Although the brandy makes it strong, the addition of the raspberries and other fruit gives this a holiday flair. For a celebratory touch, serve in sugar-frosted glasses.

Combine the soda water, champagne, brandy, peach, and raspberries in a large punch bowl. Add sugar to taste and serve in glasses over cracked ice.

Makes 2 quarts

1 pt. bottled soda water
1 qt. dry champagne
1 c. brandy
1 peach, quartered, or 1 pear, peeled and quartered
½ c. fresh raspberries
¼ c. sugar (or to taste)

SUGAR-FROSTED GLASSES
RUB A LEMON, ORANGE, OR LIME WEDGE OVER THE INSIDE OF EACH CHAMPAGNE GLASS AND FOR ½ INCH ALONG THE OUTER RIM. THEN, POUR EXTRA-FINE SUGAR IN EACH GLASS, SWIRL TO COAT, THEN DIP THE RIM IN THE SUGAR AS WELL. PLACE THE GLASSES IN THE FREEZER TILL SERVING TIME. (EXTRA-FINE SUGAR CAN BE PURCHASED IN MOST SUPERMARKETS, OR PUT REGULAR SUGAR IN A FOOD PROCESSOR FOR A FEW MINUTES TO CREATE YOUR OWN.)

Champagne and Red Raspberry Shrub

Shrub is a sweet and tart usually nonalcoholic drink that was particularly popular at holiday time mixed with rum, wine, or, as here, with champagne. During the 19th century, shrub was made at home by soaking raspberries in vinegar, adding sugar and a touch of mint, boiling it, and then straining. Today it can be purchased from gourmet specialty sources. Mixed with champagne and other liquors, it makes an especially refreshing holiday punch.

1 6-oz. bottle Red Raspberry Shrub (available at specialty sources or by mail from The Victorian Cupboard, call 1-800-653-8033)
1 bottle white wine
1 bottle dry champagne
Fresh mint leaves to garnish

Combine the shrub, wine, and champagne and pour into ice-filled glasses. Garnish each glass with mint leaves.

Makes 3 quarts

Authentic Variation: This makes a glamorous—and tasty—addition to holiday parties. Freeze the cranberry juice and berries in a ring mold until solid. Unmold and place in a punch bowl. Pour the champagne, shrub, and orange liqueur into the punch bowl. Garnish with mint leaves.

Makes 4½ quarts

1 qt. cranberry juice
1 c. fresh cranberries or fresh raspberries, washed
4 bottles champagne
1 6-oz. bottle Red Raspberry Shrub (see above)
¾ c. orange liqueur
Mint leaves to garnish

Victorian Claret Cup

The effervescence in this classic—ever so slightly sinful in the 1870s—is part of its charm.

Combine the sugar, water, and sliced lemon in a large bowl. Let steep for 30 minutes, to dissolve the sugar. Add the champagne, sherry, and Bordeaux. Stir thoroughly. Serve in tall glasses over crushed ice.

    Makes 1½ to 2 quarts

¼ lb. sugar
1 c. cold water
2 lemons, sliced
2 c. champagne, sparkling white wine, or *methode champenoise*
1 c. medium-sweet sherry
1 qt. claret or Bordeaux wine

Yuletide Fruit Punch

This bright, peach-red nonalcoholic fruit punch, based on an 1898 recipe in *The Enterprising Housekeeper,* is very sweet, and if you use a juicer to make the juice from fresh fruit, it is relatively easy to make.

Boil the sugar and water in a small saucepan, until a thick syrup forms. Set aside. In a large bowl, combine the orange, strawberry, lemon, and pineapple juices. Let stand 20 minutes, then strain and chill. Add the cherries. Add the syrup, diluting the punch with water to taste (start with ½ cup water and add more as needed). Serve chilled over ice.

    Makes 1 quart

2 c. sugar
1 c. water
½ c. orange juice
1 c. strawberry juice
½ c. lemon juice
1 c. pineapple juice
½ c. Maraschino cherries